ALSO BY PETER NEIL CARROLL

POETRY

Talking to Strangers: Poetry of Everyday Life

Something Is Bound to Break

An Elegy for Lovers

The Truth Lies on Earth: A Year by Dark, by Bright

Fracking Dakota: Poems for a Wounded Land

A Child Turns Back to Wave: Poetry of Lost Places

Riverborne: A Mississippi Requiem

NONFICTION (SELECTED)

Keeping Time: Memory, Nostalgia & the Art of History

The Odyssey of the Abraham Lincoln Brigade: Americans in the Spanish Civil War

From Guernica to Human Rights: Essays on the Spanish Civil War

It Seemed like Nothing Happened: America in the 1970s

The Free & the Unfree: A New History (with David W. Noble)

Puritanism & the Wilderness

THIS LAND, THESE PEOPLE

THE 50* STATES

*(plus Washington, D.C.)

New & Selected Poems

By Peter Neil Carroll

THE POETRY PRESS OF PRESS AMERICANA

LOS ANGELES | HOLLYWOOD

Published by
The Poetry Press of Press Americana
americanpopularculture.com

Cover Art: Press Americana with photographer Jeannette Ferrary

Library of Congress Cataloging-in-Publication Data

Names: Carroll, Peter Neil, author.
Title: This land, these people : the 50* states : *(plus Washington D.C.) :
    new & selected poems / by Peter Neil Carroll.
Description: Los Angeles : The Poetry Press of Press Americana, [2022] |
    Summary: "'Traveling the land,' poet Peter Neil Carroll observes
    'restless people, pulled or pushed, going places they've lost or found,
    both grieving and hopeful, looking for something. Newcomers settle in
    all states, revealing tensions both indoors and out, some kept quiet by
    custom, some easily inflamed by rapid, unwanted change.' His poetry
    encourages others with this message: 'Keep your eyes open. Be surprised.
    Strangers live everywhere. So do neighbors'"-- Provided by publisher.
Identifiers: LCCN 2022026595 | ISBN 9781735360140 (paperback)
Subjects: LCGFT: Poetry.
Classification: LCC PS3603.A7748 T55 2022 | DDC 811/.6--
    dc23/eng/20220609
LC record available at https://lccn.loc.gov/2022026595

For Jeannette

To the States or any one of them, or to any city of the States *Resist
much, obey little,*
Once unquestioning obedience, once fully enslaved,
Once fully enslaved, no nation, state, city of this earth, ever after-
ward resumes its liberty.

—Walt Whitman

I am he who walks the States with a barb'd tongue, questioning
every one I meet,
Who are you that wanted only to be told what you knew before?
Who are you that wanted only a book to join you in your nonsense?

—Walt Whitman

TABLE OF CONTENTS

PREFACE   This Land, These People   1

ALABAMA   Aliens   3

ALASKA   Landfall   4

ARIZONA   A Shoe Falls Apart   5

ARKANSAS   Sundown   6

CALIFORNIA   Backstage   7

COLORADO   Between Seasons   8

CONNECTICUT   Winter Light   9

DELAWARE   Imaginary Characters   10

FLORIDA   Spaniards of Ybor City   11

GEORGIA   The Peach State   13

HAWAII   Soundings   14

IDAHO   Morning at Lake Pend Oreille   16

ILLINOIS   Confluence   18

INDIANA   A Hoosier Woman   20

IOWA   The Big Guy Wearing a White Hat   21

KANSAS   The Road to Atchison   23

KENTUCKY   Everlasting   24

LOUISIANA   Postscript to a Flood   25

MAINE   Home Bound   26

MARYLAND   A German Touch   27

MASSACHUSETTS   A Merry May   28

MICHIGAN   Men Who Don't Drive   30

MINNESOTA   Minneapolis   31

MISSISSIPPI   Religion at the Riverboat Casino   32

MISSOURI   Mark Twain Returns to Hannibal   33

MONTANA   Little Big Horn   35

NEBRASKA   Nebraska Spring   37

NEVADA   The Last Stop   38

NEW HAMPSHIRE   Lake Winnipesaukee   40

NEW JERSEY   Hitchhiker   41

NEW MEXICO   Waiting for the Moon   42

NEW YORK   Crossing from Brooklyn   43

NORTH CAROLINA   Bluegrass on Gold Hill   45

NORTH DAKOTA   Birds of Dakota   47

OHIO   Quiet Please   48

OKLAHOMA   Tourist in Me   49

OREGON   The Old Flame   50

PENNSYLVANIA   Little Secrets   51

RHODE ISLAND   A Little Key   53

SOUTH CAROLINA   Heritage   54

SOUTH DAKOTA   Things We Missed   55

TENNESSEE   Home of the Blues   56

TEXAS   Checkpoint   57

UTAH   Plates of Steak &
                        Potatoes Sat Untouched   59

VERMONT   Northern Lights   60

VIRGINIA   In the Country   61

WASHINGTON   No-No Boy   62

WASHINGTON D.C.   How I Missed the
                        White House Tour   63

WEST VIRGINIA   Appalachia   64

WISCONSIN   Epitaph   65

WYOMING   Medicine Wheel   66

NOTES   67

ACKNOWLEDGMENTS   69

THANKS   70

ABOUT THE AUTHOR   71

PREFACE

This Land; These People

Americans take pride in family trees, a sense
of *home*—and yet the American Miracle is not
a story of roots. Our people came from elsewhere.

Passing through Bogota (bah-GO-tah) New Jersey
one morning, I helped a hitchhiker find her way
home—though her home was a half-way home.

Spaniards who came to America to roll cigars
settled in Ybor City, Florida, hoping to return to
Spain some day, but civil war came; they stayed.

Mark Twain, returned to Hannibal, Missouri,
(billed as "America's home town") to watch
Old Man River roll by; he didn't linger long.

Some homelands survive for centuries. High in
the Buckhorn Mountains in Wyoming, Native
people constructed a circular "Medicine Wheel,"

an American equivalent to England's ancient
Stonehenge, a sacred site for astronomical
observations and ceremony, still used today.

A night visitor to the White Sands deserts in New
Mexico may witness an amazing full moonrise
similar to sighting Northern Lights in New England.

In Anchorage, Alaska, an Inuit singer reminded
me that front doors do not always open, try going
around the back; just don't expect a welcome.

Traveling the land, I see restless people, pulled
or pushed, going places they've lost or found,

both grieving and hopeful, looking for something.

Newcomers settle in all states, revealing tensions
both indoors and out, some kept quiet by custom,
some easily inflamed by rapid, unwanted change.

One thing is sure: you never know what you'll find
until you're there. Keep your eyes open. Be surprised.
Strangers live everywhere. So do neighbors.

1 PEOPLE IN MOTION

ALABAMA

Aliens

It's what you can't see in Alabama,
the kid's soccer ball hidden in a shed,
someone's mama behind a curtain
waiting for sundown to go outside.

I hear the pickers fled the state,
fields red with broken tomatoes.
No cook to fry a taco—the white man
boarded up Rico's Cantina.

After the preacher went, leaving
the *Iglesias* locked, thieves
stole a silver chalice, baffling police.
All the usual suspects had vanished.

One matinee features a civil rights
movie. When it goes dark at the end,
no one, white or not, leaves their seat.
No one wants to face the light.

ALASKA

Landfall

A crowded square in Anchorage,
July sun drums on skin,
her red hem touches bare ankles,
the Inuit in moccasins singing

Lady Liberty did not greet us

Boy baby on shoulder-high cradle board
blinking black eyes, his mother listening,
a star-studded helium balloon escapes.
He naps, his mother claps. The singer repeats

Lady Liberty did not greet us

Black-braided on the whitest day, perfect
cloudlessness, the amplified Inuit sings,
the baby's awake, gripping the stick
of a blue starred flag. She sings

Lady Liberty did not greet us

Fur-wrapped and leathered, fish hunters
followed craggy inlets and coves, built fires
in shoreline caves, lived in rocky shelters.
An upsurge of great seas drowned the past.

We slipped in through the back door

ARIZONA

A Shoe Falls Apart

In the Sonora desert, nothing
is purely accidental. It is policy.
Give no assistance, kill enough
migrants, they will stop coming.

My borrowed Ford strains
to defeat heat and distance, dims
the illusion of safety. A traveler's
inclined to think imprudently
how far away can rescue be?

Far: as human coyotes steer
their prey into a scorched glare,
slow wind, thirst. Soon a shoe
falls apart, a bra strap is tied
around the sole, remnants buried
in sand with the lost, the dead.

The desert knows its business,
how to cook a body fast, tender.
Find out, step off the blacktop.

Ditat Deus: God Enriches.

No one will see exactly where
you've gone, where you stopped.
No one expects a quick return.

ARKANSAS

Sundown

I ask Wilmer, the oldest black man in the room,
who was the oldest black man he ever knew
and what did that old man teach him?

Wilmer rubs his chin, speaks softly, without
hesitation, tells us the story he's heard—

that night in September 1919 when a posse
shot into a meeting of sharecroppers
planning to start a fair-price store,
and the farmers, those not killed on the spot, fled
into the woods, and for a week the hounds hunted
them, treed the luckless survivors, whose bodies
were tossed by the dozens onto slow moving trains
trundling north and buried there by persons unknown
who also could never go home—

When he stops, we sit stock-still, numbed
by the horror, though not surprised.
Word-of-mouth keeps their history alive
and with parched voices they tell their stories—
shotguns stacked at the front door, fear
of sundown, fear of having business in town,
fear of what might happen tonight.

CALIFORNIA

Backstage

After I bought my first brown broad-rimmed cowboy hat
and came upon the 40ish, pot-bellied horse-groom, brushing
the sleek flank of his muscular Clydesdale stallion, an animal

that would be paired with another mighty creature to pull
the iconic stagecoach at the head of the Hollister parade,
I knew, Dude, how ridiculous I looked under the brim.

Horse trailers and pickups were festooned with Stars & Stripes,
the brass band was warming up to Sousa's *Thunderers March*
and a microphone across the track blared patriotic greetings.

The groom barely glanced, an amused look as he sized me up
like someone who had parachuted from Mars onto his dry
dusty field, and continued to brush the horse's luscious rump.

How many hands? I asked. Which brought a pause to his labor.
He asked where I was from. San Francisco,
I admitted, confirming his suspicion. Slowly,
without malice, he said, *Welcome to America.*

2 STAYING PUT

COLORADO

Between Seasons

Beavers cracking creek-ice announce
an early thaw, the late snowfall means
danger, more soft-melt will pour.

The path is marked by floods—broken
timber, a quartz stone dug deep into the pit
of a crooked limb, split rock, landslide.

Snow blankets the woods. I follow a fresh
trail of animal scat uphill, pass through
an opening to a white meadow—startled

by woolly elk chewing tree bark, a herd
of fifty, their spring coats mottled between
seasons. A young pair rub chins like lovers—

each linked by incestuous genomes,
the same bonding as clustered aspens clasp
a common root, and more snow falls,

drifts into shroud. Our elk remain indifferent
to catastrophe, such wild innocence, unaware
there's anywhere, any reason to hide.

CONNECTICUT

Winter Light

Heavy sky reflecting the white land, my earliest
memory of Connecticut. Stepping into thigh-
high drifts I lost a shoe, had to be carried inside,

saw flames in a fireplace, my first Christmas tree.
By morning, the wind had built walls of snow,
closed roads. My father led a caravan of cousins

across the frozen lake, dragging sleds to bring in
groceries. Powder on ice, a sudden gust stirred
a blizzard, scaring the kids. My father wrapped

a muffler over my chin and the girls cried all
the way home. I learned later my uncle Al won
his big house gambling with dice in a tavern.

Ten years pass, first death, same road to Naugatuck,
sun glaring between snow-bound trees, annoying
the eye, opening questions about Al's short life.

At 14, I felt fear, seeing a corpse, a face, his fate.
He looks, said my mother as we met the open
coffin, like he'll sit up in a minute. He did not.

No one offered me sympathy. No one had to.
I could see where I was bound by blood,
a rider in the back, my eyes on the frigid sky.

For months I saw Al's silhouette in clouds.
New England's earth had frozen shut, diggers
had to wait for spring, a burial yet unfinished.

DELAWARE

Imaginary Characters

The richest persons never go on diets,
never binge, they're pure No-bodies,
imaginary characters like Donald Duck's
Uncle Scrooge, the Disney cheapskate
who quacks with joy when swimming
in pools of dimes and dollar bills.

Hard to picture a make-believe citizen,
ghost-like, extending invisible hands,
red tooth and claw—and despite
lack of vocal cords or cranium—
expressing opinions
in the form of cold cash and credit.

Tiny Delaware is that state of mind
most sympathetic to corporate fantasies,
considers its Boards as families, passing
a legacy, culture, assets, health and wealth
through preferred stocks and bonds.

Speak no evil of their immense wealth —
they mean well—and pay no attention
to profits drawn from spills and poisons
that will live on earth forever.

Do not envy these ethereal persons, clever
as angels and who, like them, shall never die.
Remember (as the great McGuffey put it)
the rich have many troubles which we know nothing of.

FLORIDA

Spaniards of Ybor City

Asturias is a poor country,
the land stingy, its fish fickle.
One person more desperate
or more courageous departs
for America and sends a message home—
Come soon--and one left behind,
who already lost hope of finding work
to support a family, follows.

Their destination is Ybor City,
hub of Tampa cigars, welcoming
workers who can roll tobacco
into fruits that will smolder
at the end of the best meals.
Their skill brings rewards,
encouraging promises
to Mama and Papa, to whom
they write at least once a year,
saying some day they will return
to Asturias with a nest egg.

They are surprised, then, even
angered when they hear
a civil war erupts in the new republic
of Spain. Many Ybor adventurers
and their sons who speak American
volunteer to fight against rebel
generals, while more cautious ones
read newspapers closely and send
cans of condensed milk for children
trapped under bombs. When the priest
criticizes such unholy conduct,
they stop taking communion.

In the end, of course, history wins,
fascists win, and the man named Garcia
who runs Ybor's Asturian club
that flies two flags—American
and defeated Republican—goes to the roof
and saws down both flagpoles

no fascist banner will fly in Florida,
the gesture that means
he can never go home.

GEORGIA

The Peach State

Life's not too peachy for my pal
George greeting me at Savannah
airport, telling why we can't stop at
a bar: *Your hair's too long, not safe.*

He's junior faculty at a local college,
obliged to make compromises—
suits and ties, perfect courtesy for
the men who hold his academic future.

He had plans to write history books,
they were looking for good teachers.
I'm a damn good teacher, he brags, but
if they come in stupid, they leave stupid.

Truth is, he doesn't mind. He prefers
students to his colleagues. He knows
it's time to start writing, tempted not
to. *I don't know if I ever will*, he admits.

His home life is benign, unlike his first
marriage to a swinger who left him in
a sweat. Second wife he calls Queenie,
she keeps house, gardens, bakes, crochets.

The two are self-contained, satisfied, ready
to fill empty rooms with children. One is on
the way. A basset hound sleeps by the fireplace.
A cat curls on a couch. All they want is safe.

HAWAII

Soundings

We're taping sound waves at Waikiki,
catch the hiss of sharp winds whipping spray;

white crinoline running in, clap and roll,
slap on the black shore.

When it's done, we'll play the sea
on the radio, accompany a true story
fifteen seconds, maybe twice

as a requiem opens and closes
the gates of paradise.

The drone of an airplane intercedes.

Beginnings are always uncertain.

We wait for the ripples to settle
and lose the call of a passing gull.

We wait for its mate. The sky
stops shivering, the director shrugs.

We wait for the woman in the parking lot
to slam the door, her chatter continues
down the beach.

A second bird, a third refuse to speak.

Forget the bird, the director calls.

Ready: The waves comply,
lash the jetty, the struggling shore.

Breakers snap like timpani.

Foam knocks the loose rock,
stops—pebbles sigh retreat.

Cut!

Endings are never so neat.

Yesterday a rogue wave swamped
the crew, a man drowned without a sound.

IDAHO

Morning at Lake Pend Oreille

Past silhouettes of Boise, Coeur d'Alene
my friend drives north into the Panhandle, arrives
at the ear-shaped lake before sunset.

The boy-girl twins jump out with a soft baseball
begin a game counting errors
until the boy loses and goes inside.

I stay with the girl, show her how to throw
knuckleballs. *Come, see*, she yells
to her brother but he doesn't.

Darkness falls fast.

I rise early to the slap of waves
on pebbled sand, alone
with fish-odor, a perch
floating on its side.

A metal-bottomed rowboat bobs at the short dock,
I lift wooden oars into the locks,
feel the fine grain in my hands.

A few hundred yards, I'm pleased
how unused muscle takes to the work,
sun rising red over pine, silence broken
only by the cry of an unseen bird.

The boat drifts, almost no wind,
deep water muffling sound, timeless—
when the hard snap of a screen door echoes.

The boy gazes at me from the shore.
Slowly I row back, uncertain
how to explain to someone so young
the feel of wholeness.

ILLINOIS

The Confluence

Here beats America's primal pulse.

Inked by underwater spirits,
the brown current pumps, whorls
shift the spinning river,
writhe in circles that fight loose,
run deeper into watery labyrinth.

Here is America's torn body,
antique as the scarred continent.

Here wild tectonic plates broke the earth,
shuddered plains—a man on horseback
felt his unbalanced animal petrify in the track—
dropped the river upside down,
flowed backward, startled the land.

Here earthquakes forebode
the next coming, how history may end.

Here lies the nation's shame:
blend of blue northern currents, mud-brown chattel,
witches swim below the murky surface;
no operatic chorus of Old Man River
can halt the retribution.

Nor will Huck and Jim,
tricked by night, fog, fear,
escape time; they missed the confluence.

Here Mark Twain's pen stopped cold.

Here's the tragedy:

this isn't about literature, yesterday's pain,
vague mysterious wounding of a nation.

Here the future reads as the human palm.

Here the forest breathes bad air; water's undrinkable.

Here the note falls due.

INDIANA

A Hoosier Woman

Dead End, the sign is bullet pocked. I drive
in circles, the Wabash river has drifted away.

A tall gray-haired woman in blue jeans hosing
her Ford pickup can't believe I'm lost.

In her garden, the Ten Commandments stand
like grave stones. She gives directions.

Miles later, at the second fork, a lone farmer rakes
winter leaves into a fire; he points me to the highway.

More miles, I meet a work crew in a tavern,
they advise a shortcut I manage not to find.

Years ago, my father met a woman in a dining car,
her Hoosier stories opened his eyes to rural beauty.

Horses, sorghum, clover—green rolling hills became
a paradise he saw only once from that moving train.

3 THIS LAND

IOWA

The Big Guy Wearing a White Hat

Sitting next to him on an outdoor bench
we wait for the rodeo to begin,
moist air reeking of animal sweat
and manure that awaken a story,
his college days in Iowa, needing
one hundred dollars to graduate.

He returns to the family farm
the day before Christmas, knowing
he can't ask for help or expect anyone
to spare the dough
but he goes to church the next morning,
sits in the last row, watching
the collection tray coming back.

After the sermon, as is his custom,
Pastor Peabody walks up the aisle,
picks up the plate, opens the doors
to stand beyond the threshold
bidding farewell to his parishioners.

The impoverished student rises quickly
to stand beside the reverend, and as people leave,
he speaks to each man directly
Do you have a job for me?
Not one has need for labor. None.
Except the very last pig farmer
who's known the boy all his life, says
Come tomorrow at 7 AM.

Here, now, sitting in 90-degree sunshine,
eager for bronco busting, hog wrestling,
barrel racing and punching cows, he sighs
and admits the worst thing he ever had to do,
was shovel that frozen pig shit,
the smell so brutal
he burned his clothing, shoes and all.

KANSAS

The Road to Atchison

Don't ask how on a hazy
morning in April I wind up
driving through Rulo (pop. 172)
admiring a grain elevator,
a red-brick church, the
Swinging Door Saloon,
riding the scenic route
south toward Atchison,
the spring-swollen
Missouri on my left, bluffs
shouldering the view west.
Ancient glaciers throw
the country into twisted,
hard-to-plough hills, a
relief from flat grain fields
that strain the eyes with
similarity, but here
the soil appears less
prosperous, abandoned barns
nestled in lichen and vine,
a Victorian manse left to rot
near the tottering silo,
and yet for the passing stranger
a miraculous field of light
and lavender, swaying cottonwoods
along hidden streams, teeny signs
of green at the tip of redbuds,
and a small cloth U.S. flag
dangling from a mailbox. I come
to appreciate why plain
women and men stopped to live
and make do in this quiet
unnamed nowhere of the world.

KENTUCKY

Everlasting

Blue smoke hangs like mist
over two frizzy-haired women sitting
cross-legged, backs against
a brick wall, savoring morning cigarettes.

Inside, chickens have been hacked; thighs,
breasts, backs weighed, wrapped in plastic.
A young mother rolls a cart past apple sauce,
two ladies stop to cluck at her four-day son.
The butcher wipes both hands on his apron.

Vanceburg isn't a tourist stop, no outdoor bench
to sit on. Who but townspeople read
the weathered plaques on picket fences,
detailed ancestry of the yellow-frame home
of a newspaper editor dead over a hundred years,
or the pool room that gave refuge
during a flood in the last century.

At the court house, a column honors Civil War dead,
deeper in the etched script, a stormy history sleeps:

*The War for the Union Was Right, Everlastingly Right,
and the War Against the Union Was Wrong, Everlastingly
Wrong.*

Such fervor—and down the block,
the two women stand up,
flip away their cold smokes, glance

toward the gray Ohio River a hundred yards away,
a tugboat stubbornly pushing against the stream
that separated slave from free.

LOUISIANA

Postscript to a Flood

Noah and his family were saved—
*   if that could be called an advantage.*
                              —Mark Twain

Trapped by insistent coverage,
aerial views of heroic rescue
and failure, the waters rising,

a woman in a pale nightgown, hair
soaked to scalp, wails on a rooftop,
as the rain falls she calls for her boy.

She calls. Newsroom advice: Stock Up
on Matches, Name Tag Your Children--
as if that will make the river stop running.

From elongated tail to slippery tongue:
nothing but that frail breastwork of earth
between the people and devastation.

Skin insulates the body, the puncture
bleeds, dark waters impersonal,
dissolve, swallow, submerge.

The river's a planetary seam,
doesn't reason or think, love or hate.
What are two people to a river?

The same as ten, ten thousand, ten million:
the wild river is everything they are not;
the Mississippi outlives every desire.

Immortality's a human misunderstanding,
the river has its own life, washes, obliterates,
this strip of earth won't last forever.

MAINE

Home Bound

An old friend had gone mute
lately but calls today to chat
about local elections in Maine.
Neutral territory, has nothing
to do with the long silence

but I play along, ask him
if the great maples are turning,
and he agrees to be distracted,
mentions the brown bear he saw
and how his skittish dog hid
under the house.

He's been on the campaign trail,
canvassing voters who hate
all the candidates. Dangerous,
I say. He sighs, his voice faint,
tongue stuttering.

My wife's sick, he blurts:
embarrassed to admit how scared
he is, what he suspects is coming,
coming fast, like first frost, two
alone all winter.

MARYLAND

A German Touch

Turkey and sauerkraut every Thanksgiving,
a German touch, ditto for Christmas. Partly
it's an annual habit, the immigrant family's
heritage, and a reminder of what was taken
cruelly, leaving a shared phantom memory.

His father lost a hand fighting the Germans,
suffered staggering rages. *Not if but when.*
Mom finally made him leave. She often ran
out of cash but when she found money
on beach-sand, they gorged on soft-shells.

Eli who seldom mentions five siblings, keeps
fond feelings for two cats—a calico whose
name he can't repeat—it's a current password.
The other, white fur with black mustache
his father named Adolf. Strange revenge.

That cat got killed by a Japanese motorcycle.
Eli, an expert on World War II battles, thinks
the accident is a form of postwar justice.
He studies tattoos to find spelling mistakes,
those errors, those scars that last a lifetime.

4 CHANGES

MASSACHUSETTS

A Merry May

Spring fever, a sunny Sunday on Boston Commons,
           the blare of a dozen transistor radios,
What a day for a day dream
           the air alive with Frisbees, aroma of pot,
Blow Up at the movies,
           first frontal nudity I glimpse in a fast-
   moving flicker
dreaming about *my bundle of joy....*

Up the road, a certain Harvard
           psychology professor, Doctor Timothy
   Leary struggles
with intergalactic visions,
           craving earthly transcendence with an
   advert jingle,
Turn on. Tune in. Drop out.

Banners, hand-lettered placards,
           noisy students crowding walkways
   chanting

       Hey, hey, LBJ, how many kids did you kill
       today?

The riot squad approaches,
           white helmets, blue uniforms, batons,
   radios, megaphones,
holstered pistols, jeeps, tear gas, handcuffs—

The kids have many things on their minds:
           the war, the draft, its deferments.

The Brattle Street theater
                        promotes a Bogart revival, launches a
            cult for *Casablanca*,
half the audience stoned,
                        half reciting dialogue, line by line.
            Bogie, the actor as outsider,
his name becomes a verb
                        for potheads, smoke rising from joint to
            nostril (down his gullet,
esophagus cancer that would kill him).

Alive in black and white, the existential hero says,
            *the problems of three little people don't
            amount to a hill of beans in this crazy world*
and marches off to war—
            Ethiopia, Spain, the French Foreign Legion
exact opposite of what the kids are fighting outside.

That war is finally over,
                        the Summer of Love has come and
            gone, Leary's ashes have
blasted past the planet Pluto, ever faster
                        into deep space. What a day for a day-
            dreaming boy—
someday you'll understand that
                        declares Bogie, as I watch time fly
                        before my eyes.

MICHIGAN

Men Who Don't Drive

Spring snow melts into puddles,
the wool mill is reborn as a tavern
like an old dog struggling to its feet.

The once-great Motor City mirrors
the mood, houses shuttered, churches
abandoned, parking lots left empty.

I meet three gray men who don't drive
much anymore, drinking pints of ale,
our first meeting since Gerald Ford days.

Light pours through weathered glass.
We're lucky to be here or anywhere,
surprised by how much has not changed.

First, the round of health-talk, kidneys,
liver, dentists, the heartbreak of loss.
How close we are to assisted living.

Life this long is the real surprise.
On the phone, they sounded dead-voiced;
in flesh alive, quick wit to cover grief.

Like the city outside, no miracle will
follow. There is no Ford in our future.
There is no tiger in the tank.

MINNESOTA

Minneapolis

Bitter winter in the City of Lakes,
a good car, a strong-hooded coat
separate life and death. Skid into
a snow drift, the cops won't find
you frozen stiff until morning.

January, February, March, even
April before the noose loosens, boots
vanish, weight of wool lifts, bare
arms appear. By May, friends may
pause to chat on leafy streets.

In the year of Covid-19, cabin fever
exceeds claustrophobia, even lawful
citizens crave escape. Masks hard
to come by, kids hang at corners
flirting; the aroma of grass drifts by.

At 8 PM a black man stops for smokes,
passes a fake bill. Cops do what they
do, cuff him, put a knee on his neck
and wait. It's hard to watch, hard to
breathe, hard to believe it never ends.

MISSISSIPPI

Religion at the Riverboat Casino

Jim and I, we could still become millionaires,
beat the loosest slots at the sanctified tables
where fortune flutters below the Natchez bluffs,

sparkling white churches, sermons of redemption,
rebirth, the second chance that comes at night,
Jesus riding a Black Jack to the perfect Ace.

Speedboats slap the river's fast-running current,
autos dip headlights down the hill, summoned to
the jingling gospel, the reprobate to tent-camp,

men open-collared in tuxedoes, women gowned,
golfers rich in ritual lift their chinos at the hips,
lipsticked ladies plant cigarettes in bowls of sand.

Each saint approaches the anxious seat, the table
where selection demands a furtive kiss to the dice,
fearlessness before all evidence of intelligent design,

the last reckoning. Praying for rebirth so they exit,
winners and losers equal, God's child confident, but
for an invisible blemish they may dwell with the elect.

Sunday morning we spot a white-pimp Cadillac limo,
satellite antennae on the trunk, two square plaques
gleam in sunshine: CLERGY-PASTOR. The heavy-set

driver emerges, leaning on a cane, limps to his pulpit.
Jim, I inquire: "Do you think the meek inherit the Earth?"
"This casino goes," he smirks, "the whole town's done."

MISSOURI

Mark Twain Returns to Hannibal

A black-tailed shore bird sails above the sun-burnt river,
the white-suited man lifts a palm to shade his brow,
watches the bird descend onto an upstretched branch
of a drifting still-green willow tree.

The fast current spins dead limbs into soft eddies,
pulling round, round, like a treading swimmer,
then bursts downstream,
past the jutting point that shutters the old man's view.

His eyes lift to the mid-river islands, wild with unharmonious
birdsong,
then further east into Illinois, searches below the noisy islands,
two miles, maybe three
where the oblique riverbend again closes the light.

Here as a boy he saw, in bits of bark and leaf,
floating picket boards, an unhinged front door,
one pine-shingled roof gored by an apple limb,
and imagined ransacked drawers, treasures, gold, pirates,
corpses.

Fantasies followed the floods.
He read his future in hieroglyphics printed
on rippling waters, scribbles of debris, searched
for opportunities, concocted schemes of escape.

Here stands Twain's snug village, crisscross of streets,
brick sidewalks, white clapboard houses, small shops,
all circled by hills in a half-moon crescent,
the stone-paved boat-landing quiet, the town in a doze.

Twice daily, the gaudy steamboat roared, steam valves
screeched,
wheels churned, sailors screamed, the world arrived—

and then in a dime's time, upstream or down,
the river resumed. Easy for a boy to crave adventure.

The white-haired man returning,
shades his brow, eyes measuring time's distance,
he's come home to reminisce,
to dream and is quickly gone.

MONTANA

Little Big Horn

The Great Spirit gave us this country as a home.
You had yours.
                    —Crazy Horse (Lakota)

Strewn like wild flowers, granite rock roots
on the withered crest, slabs of marble
summoning pilgrims to the shrines.
The soil is dry, warm to the touch,
the air clear, wind soundless.

     A'KAVEHE ONAHE
     LIMBER BONES
     A CHEYENNE WARRIOR
     FELL HERE ON
     JUNE 25, 1876
     WHILE DEFENDING
     THE CHEYENNE
     WAY OF LIFE

An old man, war buff, preaches to a boy,
pointing to the ravines of famous errors,
miscalculations, blind spots on the ridge,
the exposed flanks where cavalry shot
horses for barricades, distance from water.

     U.S. SOLDIER
     7TH CAVALRY
     FELL HERE
     JUNE 25, 1876

The kid knows the lessons of thirst,
he's sat four days in the back seat,
heard of Custer's initiative, bravery,
hubris. He knuckles sweat from his eyes,
turns away. *What's a massacre, Dad?*

Dad hesitates, thinking slit noses, scalps,
a stick pushed into each ear so those who refuse
to listen will hear better in the next world,
an arrow stuffed up the penis to teach
the General not to rape Native women.

The spectacle, spacious as mountain vista,
too grand to absorb each little horror
the one by one killing that sickens, terrifies.
Summer sun blazes the air, dry grass drinks
the traveler's tears. He has lost his voice.

NEBRASKA

Nebraska Spring

Honor to Pioneers who Broke
Sods that Man to Come Might Live
            —On the state capitol in Lincoln

Mudbound, a squadron of ducks paddles
the mucky pond, a smell of fertile water
after night rain. In unplanted fields lime-

colored grass mixes with twelve shades
of rusty-brown stubble, spacious acres
open to the planet's edge. The horizon

a full circle, blue-gray cloud ominous,
the land below endless, flat, patient.
No human in sight. Nothing moves.

On one lost farm, a rusty tractor sits in
a ditch, useless as the swinging door
of the roofless house, the barren barn.

Birdsong hidden in sycamore leaves,
oil-black soil ripening seed, and here's
the sun. Everything's ready to spring.

NEVADA

The Last Stop

*What I suffered in contemplating his happiness,
pen cannot describe.*
                              —Mark Twain

Joe calls, asks me to meet him at the annual
convention in Reno, land of easy marriage.

He is waiting in the hotel bar, hoists a glass
and the first toast of spring—*To Summer*.

What's new? My kids, and he gives a litany—
an abortion; cocaine; molestation; cheating.

Fortunately, he doesn't gamble. Reno will not
improve his life, nor worsen it. He does drink.

How's Sheila? His face flushes. It's back.
Both breasts. The crap never ends, he says.

I study his watery blue eyes. He orders Scotch.
We head to a Basque eatery, stick to the bar menu.

He falls in love with Pincon Punch, a bitter orange,
garlic fries, roast lamb. Too much. Too many.

No matter, he's stuck in the past, remembering
a lifetime of mistakes. Let's take a walk, I say.

He follows me out but has lost his focus. Streets
are dark, we need to find our hotel. He's no help.

He trudges up a ramp, thinking we have a car,
circling levels, weary, stops at a chain-link fence.

He's given up. His eyes shut, he begins to sing,
an Irish tenor, *Danny boy…the pipes are calling….*

Reno is the last stop. He calls again, sounding sad,
his wife didn't make it, his oldest son a suicide.

What can I say, what sympathy? We talk of old times,
his glorious teaching career, prizes won. He admits

the comfort of whiskey and the young Irish woman
who pushes his wheel chair, sings when she cooks.

5 PASSING

NEW HAMPSHIRE

Lake Winnipesaukee

Summers in the white mountains,
my young father spent his days
in a green rowboat, a yellow-glass rod
propped across the bow.

Nearly each day the same—at dawn,
again after noon, then just before sunset,
he made three expeditions interrupted
by three meals my mother made
from trout, perch, bass, rare bullheads.

Hours he sat bare-chested in sunshine,
pleased when I joined him,
as pleased when I didn't, hours
he gazed at the line's play
between wet and light.

I've outlived his span, but come
no closer to understanding the lure,
what he took from that pristine
solitude, besides the fish.

NEW JERSEY

Hitchhiker

Dawn, driving through Jersey suburbs, I see
a thumb wagging, brake fast, taking her in—
light hair, tight jeans, lots of mascara.

Stop here, she orders in half-a-mile, pointing
to a solitary Chevy parked at a littered curb.
Someone, she claims, has stolen her purse.

Doors unlocked, I search for the keys, find
none. The trunk is sealed. Neither locksmith
nor felon, I can't retrieve her precious cargo.

Though helpless, she's not distraught, rather
calmly asks if I'd drive her home. A poker term
comes to mind: in for a nickel, in for a dime,

but first she reaches into the back seat, saying
you might as well take it, offers my reward—
a gallon container of peanut oil. Can I refuse?

Entering the city, I break silence, ask her what
she does. *Dancer.* And I guess that's why she's
up early with so much makeup. Where, I wonder.

She names a well-known strip club, tourist bait.
I'm stuck for a response, decide not to question
her dance style, but inquire about the clientele.

Mostly married guys, she says, lonely guys, losers.
I'm surprised. My thoughts turn to my lucky self.
Just lookers, she adds. They're not allowed to touch.

Here, she announces, in front of a redbrick row house
on a tree-lined street, *My halfway house*—and leaves
me to ponder what to do with all that peanut oil.

NEW MEXICO

Waiting for the Moon, White Sands

The plaza broils all afternoon. I loiter
over cheese tortillas, lukewarm beer,
waiting for a pink flare to awaken
stone mountains across the desert,

welcoming me into shaman country—
gypsum dunes white as snowfall,
a wilderness of yucca and violet roses
bedded on crests slippery as the sea.

The full moon's expected, first
night after the longest day. How
the ancients marked this celestial
coincidence is lost. I'm on my own.

The sky blackens slowly. Venus appears,
red tinge of Mars, faint constellations.
Luminescent soil defines Earth's edge,
traces the orbit. My instinct is to grasp a rail.

Stiff winds chatter the dry branches.
A boy on another hill rattles a drum,
stops abruptly. A motor breaks the quiet.
Red tail lights fade into darkness.

Wind behind me slackens, night falters.
I turn east, hoping not to be fooled
by the fluorescent glare lifting
off the flats of Alamogordo.

Suddenly that red breath—the moon
igniting the desert turns my body
to ice, seeing in clean light
the vast loneliness coming closer.

NEW YORK

Crossing from Brooklyn

*And you that shall cross from shore to shore years hence are
more to me...than you might suppose.*
                                        —Walt Whitman

Double brownstone arches open a road
to the grand metropolis, short transit
from Whitman's Brooklyn hillside
to the jammed streets of Mannahatta.

The route's a magnet of expansive desire,
possibility, hope, what graffiti artists
repeat, as I cross over the Bridge:
Don't Live Your Dreams; Dream Your Life!

And so many lovers' notes: *Seb + Sophie,
Vetlana=Valera, Marco & Celine*—
and tens of thousands more writ and
erased with each rainfall, each blizzard.

A September afternoon, the air is crisp,
steady winds from the west dragging
distant clouds closer, the gulls away.
A helicopter taxi ratchets and grinds.

Today the East river runs fast, swarming
with tugboats and ferries and kayaks,
young muscular men racing on jet skis,
blue police boats making their rounds.

Surely, I see grifters as well—a bearded
man carrying a twelve-foot yellow snake
to charm girls or sell keychains, T shirts,
yes a thin book of Brooklyn poetry too.

And another million selfies, lovers grinning.
But no cynicism, please. The sun is real,
the air suffused with Atlantic salt, great
skylines: buildings shining on both shores.

NORTH CAROLINA

Bluegrass on Gold Hill

Plain folks in plaid shirts swarm to Gold Hill,
fiddlers bow a moaning sob, the big string bass
punches out chords, banjos swing, singing

> *I once loved a maid*
> *and I loved her so well*

Flat-feet pounding, two-tap cloggers doing
a Celtic step, heating the tempo, jumping
on the hard-wood floor, dripping with sweat

> *I don't want your greenback dollars*
> *I don't want your lock and chain*

Clapping hands, a five-year old shimmies in a metal chair,
Grandpa's smile all pride, he'd be any small-town boy
gone gray, but Haddie Jane from Maryville makes him unique

> *Swing your partner, find another couple*
> *Swing your opposite lady, find the one*
> *you brought*

A red-faced man begs for a breather, the slim dude leaps
to a woman's hand, no one drops the beat. Squires and Ladies,
gray heads and toddlers, the shy and the shameless.

> *Hardest work I ever done,*
> *Workin' on the farm,*

Somebody yells, *Where y'all from?* Someone else cries
Tennessee, then *Maryland, Pennsylvania.* I shout *California* and
hear a hush of great distance 'til someone else calls *London*

> *Easiest work I ever done,*
> *Swingin' my true love's arm*

This is real, a woman shouts as sundown shades to a new moon.
Mothers come to gather their lambs, dancers unlace their hands.
Most just weary, setting on a bench, humming in their heads.

> *Oh, I ain't gonna work tomorrow*
> *and I may not work next day*

NORTH DAKOTA

Birds of Dakota

Old Highway 2 leads to a steel fence
far off the road. Circular tracks lie in
wait for the multi-warhead vehicles.

Otherwise only hay fields, cows, a silo,
red barn, hills reaching to the sky—
a distant train of tankers freights east.

The Bomb sleeps underground, its
brain, organs, vessels hard-wired.
A gray terminal guards the software.

The officer looks at me twice, head
to toe, decides to review the story
of a farmer pestered by blackbirds:

*You see, he fired three shots
into a peach tree, a flock of helicopters
landed, soldiers asked him questions.*

I start over. At the airbase, a tour bus
passes the runway of antique bombers—
B-29, -36, -52.

Glossy white, Minute Man 2 sits
80-feet deep in concrete. Its warhead
arms in ten seconds; 1.2 megatons.

Inside war is woven: cable, batteries,
sextants; ghosts of warriors, physicists,
engineers; the air cold, time frozen.

OHIO

Quiet Please

On this autumn afternoon
in central Ohio no airplanes
buzz, no overloaded trucks
crunch gears, the loudest sound
on Main Street is a woman's voice
calling *here we are* as she pulls
open the door of the thrift shop.
Down the sidewalk, a cluster
of elderly women sit on stools
and folding chairs spinning wool,
knitting yarn, keeping alive
a culture of friendship
and purposeful labor.
Passing high school students
speak softly so as not to disturb
the trees waiting patiently to turn color
on the windless square. So still,
I hear the rattle of a key ring in
someone's back pack a dozen yards away.
No dogs bark. The birds are quiet,
squirrels do not chatter. Here the favored
tune is John Cage's silent *4`33``*
though the radio of a passing car interrupts
for ten tumultuous seconds. In fact
it's true that I see two boys "talking"
in sign language. Then a college teacher
passes my bench, her leather heels clacking
in rhythm, most everyone else goes in
sneakers, and here, coming back,
she clacks again. Across the street,
a yellow school bus looms into sight.
It must be time to leave the day in peace.

OKLAHOMA

The Tourist in Me

I'll tell you about visiting my fiftieth state
from Cimarron hills to the streets of Muskogee.
Oklahoma's a great place to get lost.

I'll show you Eufaula Lake and a hotel in Poteau
promising NO RAILROAD NOISE! not far
from the last stop on the Trail of Tears.

I'll bring my stories: twelve attempts to find
Oklahoma's all-black towns.

How I forgot to visit the art museum in Tulsa,
but found a good plate of catfish, red beans &
okra at Smoke House Bob's. And about the day

I met a stringy-haired mechanic in Wagoner
grinning as he sketched directions to Tullahassee.
There I met a black woman with an arm
of bracelets, lost on her way to Wagoner.
The waitress winked, sold us each a map.

Oklahomans agree on basics: high speed limits,
no billboards about abortion, cancer, or gambling.

Most folks struggle. Day by day,
their sweat replenishes dry fields
with flowers whose names I forget.

Remind me to tell you everything else I missed.

OREGON

The Old Flame

Portland's gray streets feel midwestern, nestled
under cloud and drizzle, small saloons the best
havens from the wet, and my pal Dave plays piano.

He's my excuse for coming, but it's Valentines,
an old flame I hope to find is on my mind. She
sells natural food in a town that begins with *The*.

February 14, perfect day to find women in bars,
I hadn't expected a marathon: Cassidy's, Metro,
Satyricon, Aldo's, Ruby Hearts and more.

We do them all. At Bogart's club, Dave meets
a lady friend who knows all about the *The* place,
offers to guide our expedition in the morning.

The rain stops, we head east, past Multnomah Falls,
Horsetail, Bridal Veil, not much further to—bingo!
a road sign—*The Dalles*, with a scruffy auto row

and a downtown grocery selling brown rice, tofu,
an alphabet of vitamin pills. I step inside, pause
to share a long stare across the counter, then a hug.

Her freckles have faded, her hair a shade darker,
she's pregnant. Right now, she's holding a mop,
says one of her goats has just peed on the floor.

A Midwest farm girl, she grew up on horses; me,
I grew up knowing beans about oats and manure,
sheep and goats, not to mention quinoa and kale.

Herbal tea she pours, a nervous look in her eyes,
not thrilled to see me: *It wasn't meant to be,*
though we can still look at each other for hours.

PENNSYLVANIA

Little Secrets

A friend invites me to her farm in Amish country,
showing off white colonial walls, shelves of pewter.

Unlike her pious neighbors, she has a flair for fashion,
expresses feminist opinions about films and families.

She is a bruised beauty, with a taste for rum.
Nothing happens that night. I sleep deeply.

She doesn't appear in the morning, but over coffee
her husband explains she wants to run away with me.

He seems amused, as if that isn't unusual.
I'm young, intrigued, wary.

That's how we bonded, Sheila and I—
little secrets.

She talks of thwarted talent, living in a city.
Out here, no one listens.

We mean no harm; no harm occurs.
I'd see them off and on.

She'd throw a party rich with local gossip, wait
for guests to leave, then complain about sexist chatter.

Before my last visit, he called to tell me—warn me—
she'd had a mastectomy but a good prognosis.

We walk through a grove of pear trees in bloom.
It's not like I'm dying, she says.

Weeks later, an election coming, she's angry,
tells me her dream about the countryside burning.

Which is how we left it
until the day her husband picked up her phone.

RHODE ISLAND

A Little Key

It was not price or money that...purchased Rhode Island.
Rhode Island was purchased by love.
                                    —Roger Williams

A pure Puritan—intense, zealous, perfectionist—
therefore dangerous, a menace to law and order.
Yes he agrees, all truth lies in the Bible,
yet questions how any leader
can claim to know the mind of God.

Impossible, says Mister Roger Williams.

Funny, how many folks are still rapt in certainty,
know which religion is true, which false;
which life is sinful, which glorious; which weapons
of mass destruction the Lord allows, which not.

Poor Roger, so scrupulous about God's will,
first forced to seek safety in colonial Massachusetts Bay
then banished from the wilderness Zion
for indiscreet dissent, obliged to go on foot
in dead winter for shelter among the Narragansett people.

He names his refuge Providence; God's providence
that carried him here, his destiny in the Lord's mind.
Free now from bigots—King and Governor—
he savors the beauty of a single conscience,
welcomes dissidents, heretics,

even indigenous heathen. Among the natives,
he dwells in *filthy smoky holes* to better learn
their language: *A little key may open a box*
where lies a bunch of keys.

SOUTH CAROLINA

Heritage

He strung a maze of clothesline from his office
window to the door, hand-written notes hanging
like laundry on wood pins. Not exactly eccentric,
he was a good-old boy, did not always wear a tie.

True to heritage, he studied weapons and tactics
of Confederate soldiers, became an armchair
raconteur of battle strategy, could parse fire-eating
rhetoric with the finesse of a low country lawyer.

But he lacked any particle of self-importance.
He dared to play football with his students. He
attended their tap parties, but preferred Bourbons
from Nelson county, of which he was a connoisseur.

He was one of us, the students, not them, who ran
the academic mills. They disliked his informality,
thought him unprofessional, unrefined, Southern.
Besides, civil war buffs seemed old-fashioned.

First chance, they let him go. He retreated like Lee's
Army into the heart of Dixie, to spare his soul, if not
his career, and refused to shed his style, the drawl,
nor accept new-fangled ideas about the Old South.

I saw his disappointment turn bitter. He grew a beard
to save face, sported a wide-brimmed white hat, spoke
kindly of dirt farmers and the Lost Cause. His charm
faded, convincing the critics they were right all along.

SOUTH DAKOTA

Things We Missed

We didn't visit Rushmore, nor see the stone facade of Crazy
Horse.

We didn't fish for trout in blue lakes
built by the Army Corps of Engineers.

We ate no buffalo steak; we ate no buffalo stew.

We didn't engage in conversation with bronze statues of the
presidents
waiting at street corners for the lights to turn green.

We watched three brown cowbirds rise suddenly from long grass
and vanish without a trace in a field of sunflowers.

Most things we missed because our senses tuned to vivid cliffs
and falls and fossil pits.

We missed the road sign
to the Lakota people's sacred center of the earth.

We could not glimpse,

       before the age of railroads, strip mines, banks,
       before territory and states,

what had flourished, disappeared.

TENNESSEE

Home of the Blues

Long time between my visits
Memphis sits where the big river bends,
kingdom of the blues. Great names—
Blues Hall Juke Joint, B. B. King's—

but ragged Beale Street I once walked
now glimmers in pink neon, piped tunes,
the Peabody featuring player pianos,
what my Mama called tourist traps.

Everywhere a merchant's palm, a sign
No Bums abounds, though thieves persist,
of course, a red-haired woman in red pants,
cash robbed, runs madly for the cops.

I retreat to the levee to watch the longest
river pour south, here a mile wide, nestled
under a high bridge shadowing moonlight
that flickers in the slow irresistible flow.

Here the river stretches from cotton fields
to cobbled streets, waters born 800 miles above
rush toward unsuspecting acres 400 miles below,
subverts the human scale.

TEXAS

Checkpoint

Tan boots delicate as doeskin,
a chocolate finger, knuckles
smooth at the holster.
Rodriguez, reads his badge
on the gray camouflage.

Driver's license, Ma'am?
Mister, she goes
I'm not driving.

Two cameras behind him,
his green glasses reflect
two behind her.

Step out, please.
Now.
The wind lifts
black fabric, affirms the ass.

Yes. His voice continues,
scratchy, lips shut against
the dust.

Air very hot, pasty, eyes
wait two drawn seconds.
Her left heel in woven sandal
pushes back, flattening
edges of sand, holds
its position. *Come,* he says
with me. Please.

An inconvenience,
this mistake soon will…
Here, this way. He watches
her dress, the other soldier
locks my eyes.

UTAH

Plates of Steak & Potatoes Sat Untouched

Relax…God is in control
                —Bumper Sticker in Salt Lake City

They were having a fight,
the young couple,
she of the yellow ponytail,
he of the ginger beard.
It was obvious even
to a stranger two tables away,
though they kept their voices low
and their hands visible
on the red-checked oil-cloth table
as twin plates of steak and potatoes
sat untouched and only she
reached from time to time
to sip from her water glass.

Too near, too far I pretended
to be unaware lest the red streaks
on his forehead break a vessel
or the serrated knife
in her right hand surge
into his chest. I stopped
eating, caught the waiter's eye,
paid and departed, tempted to wait
in the parking lot for the arrival
of a police car or ambulance.

Salt Lake City, famous
for straight marriages, low crime,
fewer out-of-wedlock babies,
twice the country's average
for anti-depressants, statistics
that will not douse the fires
of simmering lovers.

VERMONT

Northern Lights

Legally blind, old Mr. Ballinger loved
to fish at night, his hours without handicap,
using a drop line with tender hands, snaring
muscled bullheads that spasm
as they bottom in the boat.

Unable to see star light, he would
describe their patterns from memory
as I attempted to name the imaginary
constellations he saw.

Afterwards I'd row our evening catch to the pier
near his cottage, and he'd invite me in to play
checkers. With nimble memorized finger
jumps, most often he won.

Leaving late near the end of summer,
a wild explosion of sparks ignited the windless sky,
brilliant flames that split the air.
I yelled for Mr. Ballinger, pulled him
by his sleeve onto the porch.

The carnival of starlight made him
burst out laughing, his mouth agape,
shaking the buttons of his flannelled belly,
and I wondered what menagerie
he thought he saw.

VIRGINIA

In the Country

Through mountain shade the river James
glides toward stony rapids.

The slatted swinging bridge gives
a clean view of dark-ribbed bottom sand

where spring-born turtles flail jelly legs
like babies on their bellies

and amphibians sleep on lumber sunk
when the old crossing fell in a storm.

Minnows inch upstream undisturbed
by the ripples of a hurrying canoe.

The river town whispers tranquility.
Flour mills are gone, store fronts vacant.

At the Buchanan theater, a camera man
shows me the hidden entrance for Coloreds

leading steeply upwards to a dark heaven,
six chairs next to the antique projector.

Beyond city limits, folks live as they have to,
blue TV light flickering from mobile homes.

At midnight, a dim bulb burns in a garage.
Dog's ears quiver, cats out hunting.

A brown bear walking on the yellow stripe
waddles closer to the woods.

Big Jupiter gleams through a window.
An old couple undresses for bed.

WASHINGTON

No-No Boy
                For John Okada
                (born Seattle, 1923-1971)

He returned from war
not to boast about medals
earned

while his folks were impounded
or how Japanese GIs
freed Jews at Dachau.

He knew how many died
at Salerno, Monte Cassino,
Anzio, Bruyères, the Vosges.

He lived their motto,
Go For Broke
and wrote his story

about the ones who refused
to give unconditional loyalty,
answered the inquisition

No and No
knowing they were right,
history showed.

He wrote them into blank pages
no reviewer praised
no editor wanted another look.

Such unrequited love
and loss, his widow burned
his second book.

WASHINGTON, D.C.

How I Missed the White House Tour

My first trip to DC with street-corner
pals, the Memorial Day weekend,
someone's cousin is throwing a party.

At the depot we huddle, waiting for a guy
with a goatee who for three dollars each,
promises to return with pints of rye.

Once aboard, he shows me a small book
titled *Howl*, points to the word *fuck*
in actual print. I am really impressed.

America go fuck yourself....I make friends
reading the poem at the party but the girl's
furious father grabs my hair, kicks me out.

I'm 15 years old, stuck in this pink driveway
with Allen Ginsberg, the poems, feeling dizzy.
Something my Dad used to say comes to mind.

Treat him like a man and he'll act like a man.
The idea inspires me. I light a cigarette, trying
to figure out just what a man would do now.

WEST VIRGINIA

Appalachia

The man standing at the riverbank
with squinty blue eyes tells
me how to find everything
he's lost. Scratchy voiced, pointing
a crusty finger
like a needle knitting
through thickets,
he weaves the route:

First to Cousin Jack's barn,
near the yard where the collie sleeps
and across a narrow bridge
by the broken white fence
where Dave's truck flew off
leaving his Jeannie
and the two baby girls. Turn
at the gray-stone post office.
Can't miss it. Just opposite
Frank's busted Ford that needs a motor,
he's waiting for the government check.
Now if you see the church, fresh-
painted white, you've gone too far.
Turn back in Sharon's drive,
she don't ever mind, her boys
left these parts years ago.

On the way, I pull over in a clearing
to look at a windfall of leaves,
swirling off sycamore, hickory, oak—
the way a child turns back to wave—
the mountain stripped at the ridge.

WISCONSIN

Epitaph

On a windy hill above wide plains,
the blue-gray horizon shapes a full circle,
sun turning to evening ash. In a minute
the first star, but now the pink glows
under sooty clouds, far trees dark as ravens.

Here I remember my former student
Charles King Swan—"call me Chuck"—
asking if he might correct the history
of his people, Wisconsin's Ho Chunk.

He quotes old chief Neopit, second son
of Oshkosh, *We will not consent
to the sale of any more land. . . .*
He quotes Black Elk, Oglala holy man,
Only crazy men would sell Mother Earth.

Here's the sacred land he described
and when I search for his stories
I find his name on page one in the news,
his obituary yellow as autumn grass.
Too late to say thanks for his insight.

Dr. Chuck, I last saw riding a bicycle.
His spirit inspires my travels. History,
myth spun tight with prairie and plains:
the importance of knowing *where*.

WYOMING

Medicine Wheel

What else could they do in deep darkness
but study the stars, stitch light into stories?

Holy ones spurn food and sleep, step into
into trance, seeking prophecy or luck.

The same lure brings saints and fools
to kneel at the rim, tie gifts to the wire—

herb pouches, bundles of sticks, arrows.
A buffalo skull leans on a ring of stones.

Simmering light fills the eyes with tears.
In time the wind shreds every prayer.

A hawk hangs. The body locates its fear—
being turned, falling from the planet.

I look down, seeing sun mirrored on a stone,
lift the jewel, warm in hand, place it on a rock

                        —afraid to say why.

NOTES

ARIZONA: *Ditat Deus*: God Enriches is the official motto of the state of Arizona

ARKANSAS: Wilmer speaks of the infamous massacre in Elaine (Phillips County), Arkansas, in October 1919.

DELAWARE: The quote is from William Holmes McGuffey, the leading educator in Jacksonian America, from his story "The Poor Boy," in *Newly Revised Eclectic Second Reader* (1848); reprinted in Edwin C. Rozwenc, *Ideology and Power in the Age of Jackson* (1964).

FLORIDA: For more about the Spaniards of Ybor City, see Ana Varela-Lago's "We Had to Help: Tampa's Response to the Spanish Civil War," *Tampa Bay History,* vol. 19, no. 2, 1997.

ILLINOIS: The Confluence marks the joining of the Mississippi and Ohio rivers just south of Cairo in Fort Defiance Park.

LOUISIANA: The epigraph by Mark Twain comes from his book *Letters from the Earth.* The reference to "the frail breastwork" is from his *Life on the Mississippi.*

MASSACHUSETTS: The "Daydream" lyrics were written by John Sebastian, released in 1966, and performed by the Lovin' Spoonful.

MICHIGAN: No Ford in the future; no tiger in the tank refers to auto advertising in the 1950s. See Nelson Algren's comments in *The Man with the Golden Arm.*

MINNESOTA: The confrontation of George Floyd and the Minneapolis police during the spring of 2020 lit a fire in the movement for racial justice. The subsequent conviction of a police officer for murder seemed to vindicate the Black Lives Matter movement.

MISSOURI: Mark Twain returned to Missouri in 1902 to receive an honorary doctorate from the state university and to visit his home town, Hannibal, for the last time.

MONTANA: On June 25, 1876, while most Americans celebrated the nation's Centennial, the U.S. Seventh Cavalry Regiment, led by Lieutenant Colonel George Armstrong Custer, challenged a force of Northern Cheyenne, Lakota, and Arapaho warriors led by Sitting Bull and Crazy Horse in the Battle of Little Big Horn. The crushing defeat of U.S. soldiers is also known as "Custer's Last Stand."

OHIO: The innovative composer, John Cage (1912-1992), known for his piece of four minutes and 33 seconds of complete silence.

RHODE ISLAND: The quotes can be found in Perry Miller, *Roger Williams: His Contribution to the American Tradition* (1962). Williams's *A Key to the Language of America* was published in London in 1643.

WASHINGTON: John Okada's first novel, *No-No Boy* (1957) addresses the problems Japanese Americans faced after their incarceration in government camps during World War II. After his early death, his widow tried to interest publishers in his remaining work. Failing that, she burned all his writings, including a second novel.

WYOMING: "Medicine Wheel" in the Buckhorn Mountains (elevation 9,642 feet) is a pre-historic sacred astronomical site built and maintained by Native Americans.

ACKNOWLEDGMENTS

A Child Turns Back: "Appalachia"; "Checkpoint"; "Everlasting"; "Little Big Horn"; "Medicine   Wheel"; "Waiting for the Moon"

Arkansas Review: "Confluence" reprinted in *Down to the Dark River*

Cultural Weekly: "Hitchhiker"; "The Old Flame"

Earthspeak: "Epitaph"

Fracking Dakota: "Birds of Dakota"; "Tourist in Me"

Freshwater Literary Journal: "Northern Lights"; "Lake Winnipesaukee" (orig. title, "The Lake")

HeARTjournalonline: "Aliens" reprinted in *Verse Daily*

Natural Bridge: "Nebraska Spring"

Pacific Review: "Things We Missed"

Plainsong: "Road to Atchison" (orig. title, "South of Rulo")

Radical Teacher: "Sundown"

Riverborne: "Mark Twain Returns"; "Postscript to a Flood"; "Religion at the Riverboat"

Southern Quarterly: "Heritage" reprinted in *Project Muse*

Talking to Strangers: "Crossing from Brooklyn"; "Imaginary Characters"

The Aurorean: "Home Bound"

THANKS

This collection of poems reflects my lifetime of travel around the States of America and views the state of America today from the perspective of a poet and historian. When a friend questioned why I included Washington, D.C. but not Puerto Rico, my response was that I have not visited the island but have seen and slept in all 50 states.

None of this extensive travel would have occurred without the enthusiasm of Michael Batinski, with whom I shared adventures along the Mississippi, Ohio, Missouri, and Kenai rivers and in many nooks and crannies far from my home in northern California.

My cluster of Saturday morning poets has surely improved the writing on the page, for which I thank Terry Adams, Mary Bailey, Anne Cheilek, Esther Kamkar, Lisa Rizzo, Lee Rossi, as well as colleagues Charlotte Muse, Casey FitzSimons and Muriel Karr.

I'm especially grateful to the judges at Prize Americana who awarded me for the second time. Thanks again to Executive Director Dr. Leslie Kreiner Wilson who created the cover design and encouraged this work forward.

This book is dedicated to my partner and wife, Jeannette Ferrary, still the best poet in the room, an excellent photographer, culinary writer, and my favorite editor.

ABOUT THE AUTHOR

This Land, These People, Peter Neil Carroll's eighth book of poetry is the winner of the 2022 Prize Americana. In this pathbreaking collection, he takes the reader on a fascinating transcontinental journey from the Maine woods to the Arizona border, from a California rodeo to the cigar capital of Florida—taking in all 50 states (plus Washington, DC) with personal adventures, historical background, and surprising discoveries of the state of the nation.

Carroll has studied, taught, and written about Americana both as poet and historian. His previous collections include *A Child Turns Back to Wave: Poetry of Lost Places*, which also won Prize Americana; *Fracking Dakota: Poems for a Wounded Land*; *The Truth Lies on Earth*; and an earlier volume, *Riverborne: A Mississippi Requiem*, that explores the lonely world of America's great river.

His poems have appeared in many journals and online publications. Carroll has also published over twenty books, including the memoir, *Keeping Time*. He has taught history and American Studies at Stanford, Berkeley, the University of Minnesota, and creative writing at the University of San Francisco, hosted "Booktalk" on Pacifica Radio, and edited the *San Francisco Review of Books*. He is Chair Emeritus of the Abraham Lincoln Brigade Archives and editor of its quarterly journal, *The Volunteer*. He is currently Poetry Moderator of Portside.org and lives in northern California with the writer/photographer Jeannette Ferrary.